This book belongs to

_ _ _ _ _ _ _ _ _ _ _ _ _ _ _

Problem-Solving Ninja

By Mary Nhin

Pictures by
Jelena Stupar

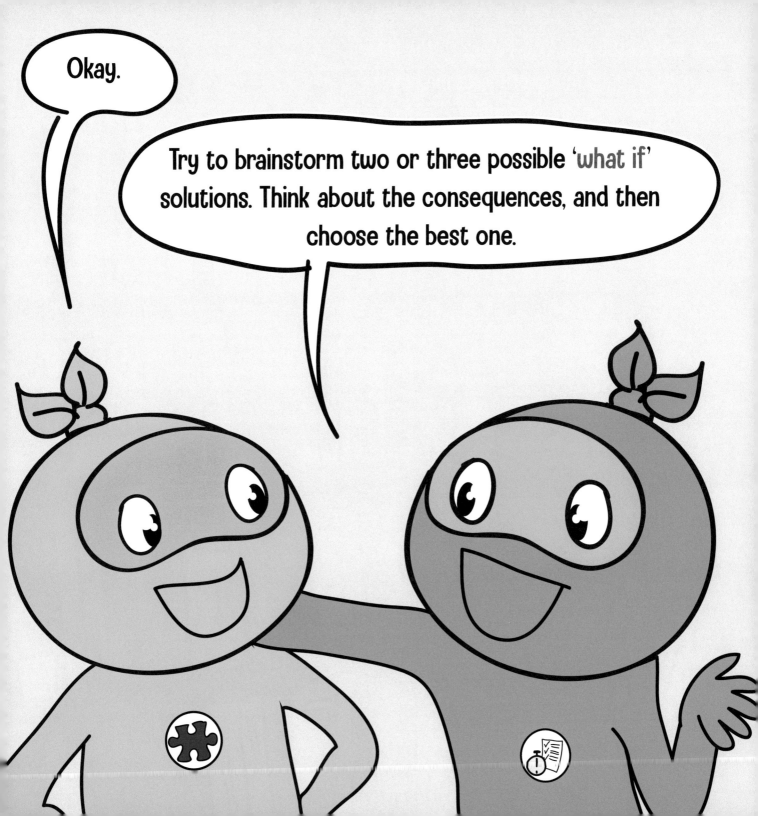

In school the next day, I went to the library.
I quickly found my favorite author, but the
books were on a high shelf.

I thought about just getting a different book. But if I did that, I wouldn't be able to read the book I really wanted, so I thought again.

I looked around. There was a step stool nearby.

I was headed to get it, but then I considered the consequences. *It's possible I'm not allowed to use it, or I might fall.* Then, I thought of an even better solution.

What if I asked someone to help me?
I saw a librarian across the room.

Later in class, the teacher began to tell us about the science fair. I didn't know what I would make. I began to worry.

But then I thought, *What if I asked my teacher if she could suggest some ideas?*

I raised my hand.

Yes, Problem-Solving Ninja.

My teacher looked at me for a moment. Then she said...

The whole class said, "Ew!" which made the teacher laugh.

Remembering the question, 'what if' could be your secret weapon in developing your problem-solving superpower!

Visit ninjalifehacks.tv to download the activity bundle for Problem-solving Ninja.

@marynhin   @GrowGrit
#NinjaLifeHacks

Mary Nhin   Ninja Life Hacks

Ninja Life Hacks

Identify the problem.
Use 'what if' statements to brainstorm solutions.
Think about the consequences.
Choose the best solution.
what if....?
?
?? ??
? ? ?
?

Made in United States
Troutdale, OR
09/07/2023

12708096R00021